THEATRE PROSPECT

TYRONE GUTHRIE

WISHART & CO
LONDON
1932

THE ADELPHI QUARTOS

THEATRE PROSPECT

CONTENTS

LIST OF ILLUSTRATIONS

THEATRE PROSPECT

LONG, long shafts of light stretching down from the gallery of the Lyceum ; dimly are seen the hundreds of up-turned faces, row upon row of white empty discs—like the key to an engraving of some Victorian Royal Christening. Dimly is seen the outline of the pro-scenium arch, like the opening of some immense Victorian tunnel-fireplace, and inside, where the grate should be, the beams of light converge. From the gallery they seem to be focussed on a tiny gaudy insect—exquisitely jewel-bright. From lower down the insect is recognisable as Miss Kitty Reidy in the charmingly preposterous attire of Prince Charming.

She is in the " Palace Garden," or is it " The Grounds " ? At all events, at the back, up some rustic steps, there is a lake. Splendidly twining forest trees overarch the scene, of which the trunks are clad in wistaria, mimosa, hollyhocks, and other bright rambling plants. The garden is bathed in a light of that Reckitts blue which electricians call Moonlight. " I bring a Song," trills Charming, in the beams. " Only a Love-Song—shy as a day in Spring."

During the third encore I allowed my attention to wander to the auditorium. The faces were spellbound—their eyes, bright in the reflected light of the stage, were fixed ; their jaws hung happily open as if they were hearing through their mouths. Next to me sat six elderly Girl-Friends—the Lyceum panto was their annual theatre treat. They were holding hands, sharing the romance.

Once at *Peter Pan*, at an evening performance, when there were few children present : " Do you believe in fairies ? " said Peter. " Yes," sobbed Clubmen of sixty. " Yes," shouted divorced stockbrokers. " Yes, Yes, Yes," echoed Hunting-women in their hard-bitten soprano tones.

I believe that it is this relation between the stage and the audience that constitutes the essence of " Theatre."

Be the performance never so good, it does not fully come alive until

B
9

an audience sees it. A live performance does not consist of certain events happening on the stage ; it is the impression which those events create upon the audience ; and the response of the audience received again immediately by the performers—a thread stretched from the stage into the front and back again onto the stage. Peter Pan may have called out more movingly at a rehearsal ; at a rehearsal Miss Reidy may have borne herself even more gallantly. Yet in either case the performance was incomplete without an audience to receive the impression and respond to it.

I

ANALYSIS OF RELATION BETWEEN STAGE AND AUDIENCE

This relation, in the first place, is reciprocal. And here is a cardinal difference between the theatre and the cinema or radio. Spectators of a film, listeners to a broadcast, receive an impression from a machine, but their reaction affects only themselves. It is very arguable that the reciprocal relation is not a good thing. The reaction of the audience, even when it is exactly what is intended, is often disturbing to the concentration of the artist. A tragedian, moved by the emotion of his audience, may easily be tempted to over-emphasis. A comedian, encouraged by laughter, is nearly always beguiled into exaggeration. On the other hand, it is only by the feel of an audience in front of him that an actor can obtain the perfect timing of a line or a piece of business. And only in the theatre can there be established the spontaneous, personal relation between the artists and the audience, varying with scarcely perceptible technical, but quite considerable psychic variation, from performance to performance. For my part, I believe this reciprocity to be essential for the full enjoyment of comedy or pathos or the emotional side of tragedy ; detrimental where the desired impression requires intellectual concentration.

It may be remarked that the reciprocal relation between audience

and actor affects not only the emotional quality of the performance but also the intellectual conception of the artist. Two instances may make this more clear. In a production of Pirandello's *Six Characters in Search of an Author*, the actor who played the part of the theatrical manager, while intelligently aware at rehearsal that his part supplied the main element of comedy in this strange play, was quite unprepared for the loud and prolonged bursts of laughter that greeted his first-night performance. Immediately he was able to adjust his conception of the character and its relation to the play, and to enrich his performance in a way that would have been impossible without the immediate presence of an audience. Again, in another play, through no fault of his own, an actor was being laughed at in situations that were intended to be serious and pathetic. In earlier scenes he had alienated the audience's sympathy from the character, so that, though he played the pathetic scene excellently, his misfortune excited not pity but derision. The danger of the scene was not apparent at rehearsal, although it had been watched carefully and expertly criticised. But, in the light of the audience's reaction, it was easy to make readjustments. The earlier scenes were differently played, the character retained the audience's sympathy, and the actor had no difficulty in making his pathetic scene have the proper effect.

Conversely, it is often apparent in the cinema that the reaction of the audience has been misjudged. For example, the pause which follows a comic line may be timed exactly right for the laughter on Monday, be too long on Tuesday, and too short on Wednesday. Or again, the portrayal of an Indian fakir may be suitably romantic in London or New York, but merely ludicrous to the film fans of Allahabad.

I should like here to note a fact which I have observed with interest, and about which others have corroborated my observation. It is not till a play is performed before an audience that the plot really emerges. At rehearsal the company works to make it clear, underlining this or that motive, picking out lines or business that make it easy for the spectator to follow the story. Yet, if one is a solitary spectator at a rehearsal, the plot of a play does not easily engage one's attention,

even if the whole piece is played through without checks. This, I think, is because one is following it alone. The producer and other technical people who may be in front during a rehearsal are not occupied with the complete story of the play, but with the technical details of its preparation. But as soon as an audience is present, following the clues together, then the plot takes its place as the main channel, up and down which are moving the waves of sympathy and co-operation between the audience and the stage.

This suggests that the relation between performers and audience is essentially sociable. What King Ludwig of Bavaria saw, alone at the opera, was not a performance but a dress rehearsal. And, being social, the relation demands certain social obligations of the guests as well as the hosts. Those who are bored ought to conceal or conquer their boredom, not out of consideration for the artists who are paid to entertain so much as for their fellow spectators who have also paid for their seats. A hostile, or restless, or listless member of an audience has the very same demoralising effect as a similar guest at a party. Because one has paid for a seat in the theatre one is not absolved from the social obligation to co-operate in making the performance as successful as possible. Payment gives one the right to be critical ; and the more critical an audience is, the more will it stimulate intelligent performers. And, if the performance is so bad that one cannot criticise without boredom, payment gives one the right to walk out. Unfortunately, it is just those people who are least able to criticise who expect a theatrical entertainment to exist without co-operation from themselves.

The sociable relation between stage and audience is affected, just as is a party, by conditions of space and numbers. The big entertainment—*Ben Hur*, *Cavalcade*, a Military Tattoo—tends to be interesting for its mere bigness and the efficiency of its organisation. It requires little else to hold the attention and its size makes little else possible. And, similarly, a big audience can generate strong mass-sensation with comparatively little stimulus, because, provided that all are fully participant, an impression becomes increasingly stronger as the number of participants increases. But then distractions increase

with increasing numbers and full participation becomes increasingly difficult. On the other hand, as at a big party, mere multitude can successfully conceal the rudeness and mitigate the demoralising effect of the non-co-operators.

The carrying power of the theatre is strictly limited. One could not expect a high level of concentration from the back rows when Miss Ruth Draper was performing in the building which is known as the Golder's Green Hippo. Cinemas have this advantage over theatres : that they can be enormously larger, while still enabling all to participate fully ; thus increasing not merely the box-office returns but the emotional possibilities of the entertainment.

At the same time, I must admit that I have not yet been to a cinema, whether great or small, where the audience has contributed to, rather than detracted from, the interest of the film. And this comparative lack of stimulus from one's fellows in the film audience is the price that has to be paid for the convenience of arriving and leaving at any hour. Concentration upon the entertainment is perpetually being frustrated, physically by the ceaseless turmoil of arrival and departure, spiritually by the fact that a large portion of the audience, having arrived in the middle of a film, is unable to follow it intelligently.

It is a rather damning reflection upon our character that we should prefer our entertainment so arranged that we can arrive and leave at any hour we please, despite the consequent detriment to the entertainment. And it is, I think, a very sinister sign of the times that the " Non-stop " principle has invaded the theatre. Already there are not only non-stop variety performances, but also non-stop programmes of one-act plays ; and their apparent success encourages the fear that very soon no management will dare to offer any entertainment that does not contrive to be continuous. For with alternative casts and revolving stages the practical difficulties are by no means insuperable.

This is symptomatic of how the economic pressure of the cinema can compel the theatre to abandon principles which differentiate it from the cinema, and even those which raise it above the cinema. For, even apart from the added possibilities of concentration, members

of an audience who have assembled at a given hour to witness a particular performance are enabled to form a more satisfactory relation both with one another and with the performance.

In the first place, the mere fact that they have taken trouble to arrive in time, taken trouble to create the relation between themselves and the performance, makes the reaction more valuable. For one values something created by oneself largely in proportion to the trouble of its creation. For instance, the flowers one has grown oneself are valued above bought flowers, one's own child above the adopted child—because the trouble is an expression of oneself. Furthermore, the effort to arrive in time tends to make one determined to have that effort rewarded by enjoyment ; also it tends to make one physically and mentally alert.

In the second place, the mere fact that an audience has assembled to see a particular performance means that audience and performers are sharing in a creative act, and this always gives a certain thrill to a theatrical performance, creates a certain tension. There is, for instance, the possibility of technical error—the curtain may stick, the leading lady may forget her lines or drop down dead. Incidentally, one of the great charms of the theatre lies in watching the company grapple with their technical problems ; finding that the leading lady . does remember her part ; that the lights do not fuse ; that the bevy of Pretty Girls actually does break out of the Monster Easter Egg. And I think it is the case, that the technical feats of the cinema, though often more difficult, do not excite the same interest because one is not actually present while there is a possibility of their failure. Then too, in the theatre, the artists are creating a given performance for an audience which has assembled especially to see that particular performance ; and similarly, each member of the audience is having this performance created especially for, and, in some slight degree, by himself. This could only happen to a very modified extent at the non-stop theatrical show, since it is only by luck that a member of the audience sees the whole of such a show consecutively ; and it can never happen in the mechanical performance of the cinema film. It is peculiar to the theatre that the relation between the stage and

the audience is not only reciprocal and sociable, but mutually creative.

It is the realisation of this that gives the peculiar thrill of anticipation to a theatrical performance. We are conscious that behind the curtain they, too, are preparing for the same event as ourselves. The scene that we shall see is being set. The lights are being focussed to illumine it for us. For us the ingenue is putting on her curls. For us the crimson Hussars are polishing their boots, the brigand chief is spraying his throat ; the pianist giving his " A " to the violins ; the clarinet giving those little bubbling runs that make of anticipation an ecstasy.

Compare the opening of a cinema, at some dead and dismal hour of the morning when decent people are at their work. The lights go out, there is a click and whirr of machinery, and the flickering images of the screen remind us that, a year or two before, across an ocean and a continent, they " made a picture."

Finally, this relation between stage and audience can vary greatly, not merely in intensity, but in quality. It can be more or less intellectual, more or less sensuous. Compare, for instance, the relation which is established between players and audience in Congreve's *Love for Love ;* Sardou's *La Tosca*, or Ziegfeld's *Follies*. It can be more or less personal, more or less abstract. Compare the intensely personal relation of a music-hall artist with the audience—Miss Gracie Fields, for example—and the abstract content of the expressionist play. More subtly, consider the psychophysical bond that endears Miss Fields to her public, and then remember that Miss Gloria Swanson is no less admired for a charm merely imaged in rays of light projected through a band of celluloid. But all this is rather in the province of the psychologist than of the student of the theatre. The latter is less concerned with the quality of this relation than with the fact of its existence and with practical methods of creating it.

II

RELATION BETWEEN STAGE AND AUDIENCE IN "NON-POPULAR" PLAYS

THIS relation is easily created in popular entertainment, but now, as always, the chief problem of the serious theatre is how to create it in non-popular plays. It is obvious that in the theatre, as with any other art, popular taste is no criterion of merit ; and the best plays, whether new or old, are seldom popular. In most arts this is only a financial problem. Given money, writers, painters, sculptors can produce their work, and it can be fully enjoyed by those few who have a taste for it. But subsidies alone cannot keep a theatre alive. Money can hire the best artists to provide careful productions of the best plays. Money can buy advertisement to persuade a gullible public to go and see these productions ; but no amount of money can persuade an audience sincerely to enjoy what is not to its taste. And I maintain that without that spontaneous, sincere appreciation, without the proper relation between stage and audience, no production can fully come to life. This seems to be the " catch " in several well-formulated proposals for a National Theatre. They make provision for good productions, but they are content to assume that because there are good reasons why a National Theatre ought to exist, therefore, granted a sufficient subsidy for their productions, a National Theatre would exist. Surely it is more honest and more sensible to admit that an intelligent theatre will only appeal to a minority of theatre-goers ; that theatre-goers, under existing conditions, are themselves an ever-dwindling minority of those who seek mimetic entertainment ; and that, therefore, if an intelligent theatre is to survive, it can only be by carefully planned organisation, not only behind the curtain but in front as well.

III

ORGANISATION IN FRONT OF THE CURTAIN

ORGANISATION behind the curtain I will discuss later on. Let us first consider the audience. The purpose of such organisation would be twofold, financial and artistic : to fill the house, and to fill it with the kind of people who want the kind of play that is being produced there.

IV

IS ORGANISATION NECESSARY?

CONSIDERATION of this requires some consideration of the present trend of theatrical business and theatrical art. First, the business. The theatre is now faced with the competition of the cinema, the radio, and the gramophone, all purveying different kinds of the same wares. As yet the radio and the gramophone have not developed the dramatic possibilities of their media sufficiently to make it necessary to regard them as more than potentially formidable competitors. Also one suspects that their rivalry will be much more to be feared by the cinema than by the theatre. Either there will always be a public for the " Fresh " as opposed to the " Canned " drama, with a sub-rivalry between " Home-Canned " and " Auditorium-Canned " ; or else the " Canned " will have won the day and the " Fresh " drama will be dead.

This victory may be achieved in two ways : either economically, or, more legitimately, by making the canned products seem more artistically attractive than the fresh. Probably it will be achieved, if at all, by a combination of the two. The theatrical situation in Canada at the present moment illustrates very clearly what may happen all over the world. Almost all the theatres over the whole

c   17

country have been bought up by American Picture Corporations. Only Montreal and Toronto have a regular supply of theatrical entertainment. Towns as large as Winnipeg and Ottawa are dependent upon local amateur " Little Theatres," which are themselves deprived of the healthy stimulus of professional competition and the example of professional thoroughness. The result is that the public, grown quite unaccustomed to theatre-going, accepts the Talkies as the only medium of theatrical expression, and young Canadians look upon the theatre much as patrons of the dirt-track regard a meeting of the Four-in-Hand Club.

Already in England the cinema has undermined the touring business and theatres are confined to a few of the largest cities. Economically, the cinema already has the theatre on the run. It is possible to exhibit films at a lower rate than theatre prices in much more luxurious buildings. Furthermore, the cinema can offer galaxies of the best-known stars in " vehicles," prepared by the best-known authors, directed by the best-known directors ; and, if that were not sufficiently marvellous, then the cinema can hire " Continuity writers " to say how marvellous it is—in a marvellous new language of their own—and, by George ! it often is ! And that leads from economics to art.

Defeated financially, can the theatre justify its survival on artistic grounds ? From its early infancy it has been apparent that the cinema could outdo the stage in the presentation of great spectacles, broadly panoramic effects. Only a year or two after Sir Herbert Tree had electrified London by producing *A Midsummer Night's Dream* with real rabbits, D. W. Griffith had made the *Birth of a Nation*. By 1911 there existed a beautiful coloured film of the Delhi Durbar, and it cannot be many more years before technicians have mastered the difficulty of producing coloured films at a rate that will make them economically possible. No detached observer can seriously suppose that the big spectacular play has the slightest chance of survival against the big spectacular film.

From its early days, too, the film has bagged the play of adventure, of hairbreadth escapes, of galloping hoofs. Isolated stage successes

18

seem to imply that the stage can do them as well, but I think that even the staunchest theatre partisan must concede to the cinema greater technical facilities for both cloak-and-sword melodrama and the modern equivalent with its gangsters and " gats " and tough dames.

For a long time it seemed that the theatre would hold its own with the " realistic " play. Let the cinema have spectacle and melodrama and romance and all the rest, the theatre would hold on to realism. And it is true that the theatre can give a wonderfully convincing imitation of real life. I suppose at the present time we are privileged to witness the very finest flowering of realistic acting ; but there are drawbacks. Some of the acting is so very natural that, unless you sit in the front seats, you can neither hear it nor see it. And, even in the most intimate theatres, the breadth necessary to make the play decently intelligible to the back seats destroys the illusion of naturalness in the front seats.

And then, along comes the cinema with Lübitsch and King Vidor ; Chaplin makes *A Woman of Paris ;* von Stroheim makes *Foolish Wives ;* and it appears that the cinema can be not only more broadly spectacular than the stage, but also reveal far more intimate detail— and, if necessary, both in the same film. Naturalistic writers and actors " do their stuff," the settings are not " naturalistic " but natural, and then the result is projected onto the screen. I must admit that to me the effect, compared with that of the theatre, is just as natural ; with this difference, that the screen pictures can be so large that they are perfectly visible, and the screen voices so loud that they are perfectly audible in every part of the house.

Actually in neither case is the effect " natural." In both, certain conventions are observed, certain concessions demanded of the audience's credibility ; and I am not prepared to admit that the concessions demanded by the film are the more exacting.

My opinions are not those of an enthusiast for films. Except for four pictures by René Clair I have not seen any films that I liked very much. But in a mass of truck from Britain and America I have seen enough to make me believe that there is not any kind of drama that

the film medium might not, in time, be able to use as effectively as the stage.

What, then, can the stage offer to justify its survival ? In my view, two things only : the reciprocal relation between stage and audience, discussed above ; and the body of drama from Æschylus to the present day. In so far as a play has been written for the theatre, and is suitable for the theatre, it is suitable for no other medium. The cinema cannot use Shakespeare, for instance, and will never be able to do so, because his plays demand that reciprocal bond between players and audience, and because in superlative degree their technique is theatrical and not cinematographic. The construction of the scenes, for instance, is entirely conditioned by the limitations of the stage. And, like every great artist, Shakespeare has turned the limitations of his medium into triumphant advantages. Illyria, a seacoast of Bohemia, a street in Venice, are all created out of the air of a theatre. They grow up round the actor while he is speaking ; and it is impossible to take a photograph of the actor and to make a record of his speech and expect the same miracle to happen, because the lines are not written for that purpose. Consider, for example, one of the great speeches from *Henry the Fifth.* The technique of the writing is inescapably declamatory ; inescapably prepared for the little figure declaiming into the big auditorium. Diametrically opposed to the technique of the Talkies, where breadth is, for obvious mechanical and artistic reasons, taboo.

Equally the excellence of their theatrical technique makes Shakespeare's plays unadaptable to the medium of broadcasting. Lyrical and descriptive passages make pleasant hearing ; but, robbed of the visual element, all the comic scenes and most of the scenes of action become quite unintelligible. Any attempt to present a play by this means can be no more than a botched-up thing—chunks welded together holus cum bolo—a mere travesty of the original.

And so it is, in greater degree or less, with every dramatist who is worth his salt. The technique of his play demands the theatre and is suitable for no other medium.

The theatre can hardly survive, however, upon nothing but classical

revivals. And, indeed, it cannot be doubted that, for many years to come, there will be writers who will prefer to express themselves in terms of theatre rather than cinema. For the cinema, retarded by the stupidities and greed of those who control its production, is being slow to develop its possibilities. It will be a long time before the notion is accepted that the film is primarily a vehicle for ideas, and only incidentally a saleable commodity. Also, even when the cinema has reached a mature stage of technical and artistic development, there will always be ideas whose expression will demand the reciprocal bond between stage and audience ; and authors who regard this as more valuable than anything the cinema can offer. Noel Coward's *Private Lives* seems a good instance of ideas of this kind. The play had no particular pictorial or literary merit. The stage picture was elegant, but unexciting. The story was negligibly slight ; the con-struction, though perfectly adequate for its purpose, showed no trace of the virtuosity that distinguished the performance. The dialogue was witty and modish, but mostly rather common. But between the audience and the four people who played the piece there existed a relation of the most rare and stimulating vitality. This I attribute to Mr. Coward's exquisitely accomplished theatrical technique. It is technique developed to the point where it becomes indistinguishable from something creative. He knows exactly how to create and how to exploit the relation between the audience and the stage ; and— this is the point—the exciting results of such exploitation both for artists and audience are peculiar to the theatre, despite the greater technical and economic facilities of the cinema.

It is often urged that the " canned " drama can never compensate for the loss of the " real " artists. This, I feel, must always remain a matter of personal opinion. For my own part I am not aware of any greater degree of " reality " in a character portrayed by a " real " artist than in a character portrayed by a moving photograph of an artist. Indeed I can recall no stage character who has seemed so real to me as the " Louis " in a film called *A Nous la Liberté*. On the other hand, it may be argued that, while a film character may well be as real as a stage character, since both are equally figments, the

film actor is less real than the stage actor ; and that the great appeal of the theatre is the contact, not with the creatures of an author's imagination, but with the vivid personalities of those who interpret them. But are not the stars equally the chief draw of the cinema ? I fancy that one experiences a more vivid reaction to the " real " actor if one is lucky enough to sit near the front. But it is a moot point whether, from the gallery of the theatre, the tiny vision of a flesh-and-blood Miss Gladys Cooper establishes fuller contact with her personality than does a monster close-up with the personality of Miss Marlene Dietrich. Contact with a personality is first of all a matter of apprehending facts, secondly of reacting to those facts. In the cases both of Miss Cooper and Miss Dietrich, only some, even of the outward facts, are available to the observer. In both cases, for instance, the observer is unable to use either the sense of smell or of touch. And in both cases many of even the observable facts have been distorted. In the case of Miss Cooper, by distance ; in that of Miss Dietrich because before her image reaches the lens of the eye it has suffered distortion at the hands of the photographer—it has been deprived of colour, for instance, and enormously enlarged. Thus one observer might claim to apprehend both the greater number and the more significant selection of facts about Miss Dietrich and, therefore, be able to feel a closer contact with her personality than with that of Miss Cooper. On the other hand, a second observer might have exceptionally keen sight, or good glasses, which would minimise the disadvantages of his gallery seat ; and might be obsessed, as so many are, with the wilderness of space that represents the cheek-bone of the close-up—the obvious disparity between the size of the photograph and the face of the original.

To the ear, on the other hand, the actual human voice at present expresses the personality of the artist more accurately than a mechanical record. But, since gramophone and radio apparatus can record human speech that is practically indetectable from the original, it cannot be doubted that, in a short while, the voices of the Talkies will be as convincing as the voices of the stage, and, just as with the faces, " closer " to the remote parts of the auditorium.

It must also be remembered that photography and recording can present a considerably idealised version of the original. Clever technicians can stress the good points of a figure or a voice, and cover a multitude of sins that would be apparent upon the stage. At the same time this process of idealisation is not without its drawbacks. There is the danger that the actor may be so beautified as to undermine his reality. There is the fact that the charm of many personalities is enhanced by the very irregularities that the beauty specialist would eliminate ; and, finally, there is the danger that, during the action of a film the camera may suddenly, and with an effect that is devastating because idealisation has made it unexpected, reveal the fact that the idol has feet of clay.

And, finally, whether or no they are as " real " as stage actors, evidence shows us that the physical or spiritual attraction of film artists is, at all events, sufficient to provoke the scenes that marked the funeral of Valentino, or the outpourings that are known as Fan Mail.

May it not, therefore, be concluded that theatrical appreciation is not differentiated from appreciation of films by the physical reality of the artists, but by the fact that the relation, created between them and the audience, is a reciprocal and mutually creative one ?

And this, as I have suggested earlier, is essential for the full appreciation of comedy and pathos. Indeed, I think it makes so much difference that on this ground alone the theatre can maintain its position in the struggle with the cinema.

But, in general, it will not, I think, be the regular entertainment of those who are interested in the drama. These will get their staple sustenance adequately and more cheaply at the " Flicks." The theatre will, I prophesy, in the next ten years become more and more exclusively patronised by those who are " making a night of it." In this they will be aided by the expense of theatre tickets. While high prices will discourage regular patronage, they will make the occasional visit to the theatre more of an adventure. For what is it but expense and consequent rarity that makes us value the orchid above the nasturtium ? Naturally the kind of show that will prosper will be

appropriate to a night out—something to go to after a good dinner. And of that sort, the kind that provides the most suitable relation between the audience and the stage—that combines after-dinner with something more personal than the Talkies—is the big leg-show with plenty of humour ; or else a light comedy with elegant ladies and well-tailored gentlemen being their charming accomplished selves— Sir Gerald du Maurier and Miss Marie Tempest in a sunny lounge hall near Godalming.

This suggests a poor look-out for the serious theatre. But adversity can be wonderfully strengthening to the constitution, and I believe that it is only through such adversity that those who wish for the continuance of a serious theatre will be obliged to face the necessity for organisation ; to face the fact that unless the public for serious plays organises itself to form some scheme for both the production and the attendance of such plays, the Theatre of Ideas will have to put up the shutters once and for all.

V

IS ORGANISATION PRACTICABLE ?

It is not possible to say definitely that organisation of an English audience for serious plays is practicable, since success depends, first upon the circumstances and quality of a given organisation and, second, upon the quality of the fare offered by the theatre in connection with which such organisation is planned. I shall examine briefly some of the attempts at audience organisation that have already been made ; suggest certain practical measures of organisation, and leave the reader to draw his own conclusions.

The evidence of previous experiments is inconclusive. The Volkstheater in Berlin and the Theatre Guild in New York bear witness to the success of audience organisation. Various English experiments have been less successful. One has failed notably and recently.

The Volksbuhne in Berlin had humble origins. Large numbers of

poor people paid tiny weekly subscriptions to a theatrical benefit club. Its officials then bargained with theatre managers for blocks of seats at reduced rates. By degrees the scheme grew. With increasing funds came the idea that the Volksbühne members should have their own theatre, with reduced prices for members, ordinary prices for the general public. This idea bore fruit in the Volkstheater, the largest and the best-equipped theatre in Berlin.

The Theatre Guild in New York opened in April, 1919, with 150 season ticket holders. By the second season this total was 500— more than double. The next year saw an increase to 1,300 ; the third year this was doubled again. Thereafter the number of sub-scribers grew like a snowball, till by 1929 there was a total of 30,500 in New York alone ; and in six other cities where the Guild sent their companies for regular seasons there was another total of 30,000.

Consciously modelled on the Berlin pattern is the English scheme known as " The People's National Theatre." Under this scheme members have to pay an annual subscription of 5s. 9d. ; in return for which they have the privilege of booking any seat in the house for half-price. There is also an Endowment Fund, with ten guineas subscription, headed by Royalty. It is also possible to become a " Proprietary Stall Member," and thereby to be assured of free admission whenever desired, upon payment of twenty guineas.

This scheme is entering upon its third season ; under it there have already been produced about twenty plays, all of some quality ; and the list of artists who have appeared in them is a distinguished one.

Upon its launching, attended by unusually excellent publicity, 6,000 members were obtained, by circular, before a single play had been produced. During the first season 10,000 more were enrolled. During the second season the membership rose to 25,000.

Unfortunately, despite these encouraging statistics, the scheme is not in a flourishing financial condition.

This, no doubt, is partly due to the fact that the second season coincided with the financial crisis. But of the vast membership it is hard to believe that there was not a considerable percentage whom the crisis induced to use this chance of theatre-going at half-price ;

so that the People's National Theatre might reasonably be expected to have suffered far less than most other theatres from the abnormal conditions. It is clear that, of the 25,000 members, only a tiny minority can have rallied to the support of the less successful productions. This means that the majority of members can only have patronised the successful shows, that is to say, the shows that were already attracting the public at full prices, where the attendance of members can only have been a mixed blessing.

This seems to indicate that unless members are also Seat-Holders their value to the theatre is very considerably reduced. It is true that the subscriptions of 25,000 members enable a theatre to start a season with a very helpful sum of capital. And no doubt it is also true that it is easier to induce people to pay 5s. 9d. down, with the certainty in view that they can, if they wish, recoup this sum by rebate on theatre tickets, than to induce them to pay a larger sum down for a season ticket for a series of plays which they have no guarantee of enjoying. It must be admitted that, all other things being equal, under the first scheme the members are getting considerably the better bargain.

Organisation of the audience has also been tried at the Embassy Theatre, Swiss Cottage, under two managements. The first was a failure. The second has opened well, but too recently to admit of conclusions.

The great handicap to any Manager of the Embassy Theatre must always be its situation, far from the centre of London, in a district rather of solid residential respectability than of romance or gaiety. It was its residential situation that first suggested the experiment of organising the audience ; but not, unfortunately, until after the opening. Inadequately heralded, both on the hoardings and in the Press, the first three or four productions were, financially, extremely disappointing. It was then, with the object of rallying the neighbourhood, that a Play-Goers' Club was inaugurated. As in the People's Theatre scheme, membership did not involve the purchase of a season ticket. Five shillings subscription entitled a member to buy one ticket per production (each play ran for a fortnight) at 1s. reduc-

tion. By the end of the first season, after about four months of existence, the club was 11,000 strong. In the next season drastic alterations were made to the price of seats. First they were raised ; then, after loud and continuous protest, they were lowered again. But under this final scale, members were shorn of privileged prices, although they retained certain other benefits—Sunday performances, for instance. At this time there was some decline in the number of members and serious decline in their attendance. For one production, for example, 1,500 members bought tickets out of a total of about 10,000. This decline was attributable, possibly, to dissatisfaction with the choice of plays and standard of performance. But the producer and company, who had been popular before, remained unchanged, and the Press notices continued to be as glowing as ever. At all events, despite one or two successes, which were transferred to the West End, the season was so unsatisfactory financially that the Manager, Mr. Alec Rea, decided to abandon the experiment, and relinquished his tenancy of the theatre.

Again, it is noticeable that, without season tickets, mere membership is not sufficient guarantee of support. And in this case, be it noted, the members were not being offered so keen a bargain as at the People's National Theatre, which was at the same time able to supply West End names in a West End theatre. The failure of Mr. Rea's experiment should not be imputed to his company, or to his choice of plays—both were more than usually good. It must be admitted that London, and especially South Hampstead, did not know this good thing when they saw it, and that, therefore, organisation of an audience was necessary. This was realised too late, and the organisation when it came was inadequate to support the theatre.

New management, under Mr. Ronald Adams, has courageously ventured where Mr. Rea had failed. The organisation is on a season-ticket basis : *e.g.* £5 buys twenty-five 6s. seats ; £1 buys fifteen 2s. seats. In addition, members have further privileges. They obtain, and may flaunt, a badge ; they have free use of the lounge of the theatre and car park ; they receive a fortnightly reprint of all

Press notices. Sunday debates and lectures are being planned, though they have not yet begun.

The response to this has been gratifying. Despite the cloud of failure that hung over the theatre ; despite the financial stringency ; despite the fact that they were gambling upon the management of persons quite unknown to theatrical fame ; 600 members were obtained in ten days. Thereafter the numbers increased steadily. A very favourable Press has greeted the first production, and business is excellent. The experiment has, at all events, made a good start.

The latest experiment in art theatre organisation in London is the Independent Theatre Club. This is a club, financed as a Limited Liability Company ; members pay an entrance subscription which enables them to buy tickets for productions. A theatre has been leased, M. Kommisarjevski will produce, an interesting list of plays is announced, and, since this organisation is a club, and since, therefore, the theatre is not in the full sense public, plays can be produced there whose public presentation has been banned by the censor. The scheme has made a successful start. Moderate publicity and the issue of no more than 12,000 circulars, has produced, within two weeks, a membership of 1,500, which is still increasing very rapidly. The quality of the productions has yet to be tested, and on that, of course, must depend the success of the scheme not merely to attract but to retain its support. The success of the initial step, however, is encouraging.

A further possible organisation is a Limited Liability Company to finance a theatre managed by the shareholders, to produce the kind of plays that they wish to see. Of such a kind is the Scottish National Theatre Society in Glasgow. A few thousand pounds were raised, mostly in small subscriptions. Subscribers became shareholders in a company which finances the activities of the Scottish National Players. Unfortunately the number of shareholders, even if they all bought tickets for every production, is hardly sufficient to make ends meet. Times have been hard for theatrical enterprise in a depressed Glasgow, that even in more prosperous days never took very kindly to Repertory. Also, with the best will in the world and the highest possible ideals,

the elected representatives of a body of " lay " shareholders are neither enterprising nor wily theatrical managers. The result is that the Company has been eating year by year into the capital and has achieved little more than holding together a brilliant little team of Scottish dialect actors, awaiting a Scottish masterpiece that has not yet materialised.

The limited liability company of audience shareholders may have advantages of financial organisation over such a scheme as the People's National Theatre ; and the disadvantages of democratic amateur management are avoidable by the appointment of a professional managing director. But there is still no guarantee of an audience being mobilised unless shareholders also hold season tickets. And, while it must be admitted that selling season tickets will not be so easy as to enrol subscription members, yet I believe it to be the more practicable scheme.

VI

SEASON TICKET SCHEME

A. Organisation to be in London

It is presumed that, in England, any attempt to organise an audience in connection with a serious theatre is best made in London. London is numerically the largest centre, and is easily the largest centre for the kind of people who, on the face of things, might want a serious theatre. However much one may deplore the centripetal tendency of modern civilisation, the remorseless devouring of her children by Metropolis, one cannot reasonably deny that it is the case. If statistics alone are not reliable, a comparison between the Edinburgh, the Exeter, the York of a century ago and their modern selves is sufficiently convincing. The process is the inevitable concomitant of the mechanisation which, again, we may deplore but cannot check.

It is true that, at the present time, a serious theatre does exist in

many of the large towns. Repertory theatres in Birmingham, in Liverpool, in Hull, Bristol, Plymouth, Northampton, and Cambridge, and intermittent repertory seasons in Glasgow and Edinburgh, provide these towns with a much more consistently high standard of entertainment than the touring companies, and provide the theatrical profession with most of its intelligent and determined recruits. But their support is only large enough to permit of exiguous salaries and an ever-changing programme, so that the performances are apt to suffer from inexperienced acting and, in most cases, insufficient rehearsal ; and in very few cases do they attain the polish of a good metropolitan production. At Birmingham and Cambridge the generosity of rich managers has largely dispensed with the necessity for box-office consideration in the choice of plays, but in the other repertory theatres there is need for a good deal of " pot-boiling." In no case is there a large enough audience organisation to guarantee ends meeting over the production of a non-popular play, and in none of the towns is there any reason to suppose the possibility of such organisation.

B. Price and Terms of Season Tickets

The estimate at a certain London theatre for the total weekly expenses of a season of plays was £550. This, I am satisfied, was sufficiently generous to permit of the plays being produced without skimping, although upon rigidly economical lines. Incidentally it is considerably larger than the weekly estimates of any of the repertory theatres to which I have had access. Mr. Rea's, for instance, at the Embassy, was less than £400 a week. But the internal organisation of a theatre will be discussed later. The point I want to make now is that £550 is a sufficient weekly estimate for a theatre to offer a programme of straight plays that, in acting and decoration, are not below the current West End standard.

Let us assume that season tickets are available at an average rate of 5s. per seat, and that these tickets are offered in groups of four for seasons of four plays, each running three weeks. The price suggested is considerably lower than the current prices of London West End

theatre tickets, and I would not suggest that seats at the theatre be available at such low rates, except to holders of season tickets, who would thus be compensated with lower prices for buying a pig in a poke.

It is very arguable that this compensation should not be too generous. First, because people support such a theatre from a disinterested, artistic motive, and would pay the full rate as readily as a reduced rate ; secondly, because too generous compensation makes the wary theatre-goer suspect a catch ; thirdly, that a cheap price makes the customer suspect a cheap commodity.

These are perhaps sufficiently strong arguments to make it advisable to compensate the season ticket holders in other ways than by reduced prices : by special performances, perhaps, arranged exclusively for their benefit, by courses of lectures, by bun-fights in the foyer. All these devices have been tried, and often with success ; but I believe them to be more valuable in cementing the interest of adherents already won than in attracting new support. Nevertheless, in this cementing of interest lies a valuable method of inducing the organised audience to support the less successful productions of a season. The more a personal interest can be fostered in the policy, the finance, and, above all, in the personnel of the theatre, by so much the less does the pig-in-a-poke element retard the sale of season tickets.

C. Requisite Number of Season Tickets

Assuming then that the average rate of the season tickets is 5s., and that they are available in books of four, each season ticket holder will have to pay £1. Then to guarantee a three months' season, at an estimated weekly expenditure of £550, it would be necessary to have 6,600 season ticket holders.

Now it is safe to assume that a considerable body of season ticket holders would also attract non-season ticket holders to the theatre— their aunts, for instance. Further, that even the least successful plays would draw a certain support from the general public ; chance passers-by, attracted by photographs outside the theatre, friends of

the actors. I believe that in practice the non-season ticket holders would always comprise more than half the audience ; and that a season that was half guaranteed by season tickets would be considered as underwritten ; and that there would not be difficulty in finding financial backing for the other half. In other words, that 3,300 season ticket holders would be sufficient to float a season.

Again, the best advertisement for a play is the word-of-mouth testimony of those who have seen and enjoyed it. The theatre that organises its supporters is automatically organising the most valuable possible publicity service. Now the weekly estimate of £550 includes something over £100 for publicity. With an organised audience, could this estimate for publicity be reduced ? It is generally believed by theatre people that big advertisement means big business, and that money spent on good advertisement cannot possibly be wasted. And certainly good publicity has many times proved to be good for business. No one can doubt, for instance, that recent advertisements of a novelty, all black and white, musical version of *Twelfth Night*, magnificently bolstered up the shaky reputation of a poor old bard, and turned what might easily have been regarded as a freakish and highbrow joke into a deservedly popular success. But then, in *Twelfth Night* Shakespeare had provided the goods ; had provided the materials for a great popular success. No amount of impudence, or wit in their advertisement, could make a great popular success out of the *Way of the World*, or *The Spook Sonata*. If the aim of a theatre is to produce popular successes and to make money out of them, then, possibly, big advertisement is indispensable. But for a theatre whose aim is to produce plays, admittedly of limited appeal, then, I maintain, advertisement expenses should be pared to the bone. If, as might happen, a production caught on, and showed promise of great popularity, then only it might be worth while to speculate on its chances, and to risk money on boosting it into a winner. But such expenditure should be regarded as exceptional and not included in the regular weekly budget. £100 a week is, by all comparisons, quite a modest allowance for publicity, even out of a total budget of £550. But if season ticket holders were forthcoming to guarantee

the expenses of a season, I believe that this amount could be defensibly—if not necessarily most wisely—reduced to half. The weekly estimate would therefore be £500 and the required number of season ticket holders 3,000.

D. *Methods of Sale*

Now, having estimated the number of season tickets required to back a season of plays, the next step is to examine the possible means of selling them.

Just as in the sale of any commodity, the first step is to persuade prospective customers that the commodity is desirable. This step has two different aspects. First, how best to create the desire in the minds of those who are not already interested ; secondly, how to get in touch with those who are.

The first is a matter of giving information, and of making it attractive but also accurate. Lying or misleading advertisement can be no less harmful from the commercial than from the moral aspect. Supposing persons to have been persuaded, by misleading information, to buy tickets for a series of unsuitable plays, their discomfited presence in the audience will not assist the success of that performance, they will not continue their patronage to another series and, worst of all, they will spread an unfavourable report amongst their friends.

The second aspect amounts to this : how to get in touch with persons who are already interested in serious plays. Lists exist of patrons of concerns like the Film Society. Some of these lists might be accessible ; and, obviously, certain fields could be more profitably explored than others—musical and literary, for example.

The second step is, having found prospective customers, to persuade them that they will not get the same commodity as well elsewhere. This must be largely a matter of creating confidence. Season ticket holders are going to be asked to buy a pig in a poke. They will naturally want as much assurance as possible that it is a good pig. They will want information (not the same information that is required in the first step to arouse interest in those not already interested, but

more detailed and specialised material. For purposes of distinction I will call them primary and secondary information.). This is difficult. Description of any work of art is difficult. Factual information is only incidentally relevant to artistic appreciation. " They measured it from side to side, 'Twas nine feet long and nine feet wide " is useful and important information about a grave but almost negligible as a description of a piece of sculpture. Yet judgments about the facts are apt to be controversial and misleading. And in the case of inter-pretative arts there is the added complication that information will be required not only about the work of art but about the performance. Also, in the theatre, not only the technical but also the interpretative quality of a performance is compelled to vary vastly in accordance with the intellectual quality of the audience. It is this, for instance, that has occasioned the decadent quality of much of our Shakespeare playing, especially the breadth and slowness of the comedy. It is this that has caused the playing of Irish comedy in England to degenerate into caricature, into the English idea of " Paddy." So much so, that on a recent tour of *Juno and the Paycock* the leading artists were behaving, to the delight of the audience, like a pair of Pantomime Buffoons. Prospective patrons of a serious theatre will wish to be assured, not only about the quality of the plays, but about the interpretative and the technical quality of their performance.

Now, how are these steps to be taken ? The first thing is to arrange for the spreading of information. The theatre is fortunate in that its activities are, to a surprising extent, considered as news ; and it is possible to get a great deal of theatrical information published free of charge in the Press. An ingenious Press agent can keep his theatre pretty constantly in the public eye, for in addition to news about forthcoming productions and the usual material of the special theatrical columns, he can get chit-chat accepted about the actresses' diet or the quaint antics of the theatre cat.

By means of the Press the whole of the " primary " information can be conveyed.

The " secondary " information will need to be in the form of sales literature. A booklet, pamphlet, leaflet, or some other nasty diminu-

tive, giving fairly detailed information about the plays, the comp y, and the season ticket facilities. The writing of the continuity he lay-out of the pages, and the format of the whole would be qu a pretty little exercise in the art and craft of salesmanship.

For the distribution of these, and for canvassing in general, the theatre might profitably take a leaf out of the book of commercial distribution, and appoint agencies in as many as possible of the likely markets, with the agents working on commission. There is no reason why it is not as practicable to have agents for the distribution of theatre tickets as for the distribution of biscuits or wine. They would receive books of tickets on the plan of sale or return, and be paid a percentage on their sales, the exact rate of which would be regulated by the law of supply and demand. For example, when the demand for tickets was brisk, the agent's commission would be lower than when the demand was slack. The same principle is in practice at present, only the ticket agencies are managed by commercial firms, instead of by the theatres themselves working through private individuals. The libraries, as these ticket agencies are called, do not, however, offer very great advantages to the manager of non-popular plays. Tickets for his theatre can, it is true, be booked through the offices of the libraries, but the clerks will make no particular endeavour to push the non-popular play, whereas they often do persuade customers to buy seats for some popular success in which their firm has an interest. Furthermore, the libraries make no attempt to canvass a particular kind of person for a particular kind of play, whereas the private agent, because his relation with prospective customers is more personal, is in a position to discriminate, to some considerable extent, between the playgoer who wishes Turgeniev and the playgoer who wishes *Charley's Aunt*.

Admittedly there is greater risk both of swindling and incompetence under a system of private agencies. And here, as indeed for the successful working of the whole plan, all depends upon the judicious selection of the personnel. But I do not believe that, given time, there would be great difficulty in finding an adequate personnel to establish agencies, not merely all over residential London, but in the

suburbs and in the towns outside Greater London, which yet princi-
pally depend upon " the West End " for theatrical entertainment :
places like Reading, Henley, Beaconsfield, Aylesbury, Hertford, and
Tunbridge Wells.

The expense of such a system would lie only in its organisation ;
the commission paid to the agents need not exceed what theatres pay
gladly to the libraries.

Such a system would enable a serious theatre to avail itself, more
fully than has hitherto been possible, of the support of the many
hundreds of serious amateur play-producing societies that have
sprung into prominence in the past few years. The staff of such
societies would often be available as agents, and the members would
be a fruitful field for canvassing.

The professional theatre is not sufficiently aware of either the
amount or the quality of amateur work throughout the country.
" Amateur Theatricals " is glibly taken to imply the production of
The Bathroom Door in a country house, or *The Belle of New York* at the
Assembly Rooms, Tadcaster. It is not sufficiently realised that, for
example, towns no larger than Newbury or Abingdon possess amateur
societies which present, not one play annually, but a series, of a
literary standard quite as high as that of the professional repertory
theatre. And these are not isolated exceptions, they are typical.
I quote Newbury and Abingdon because I happen to have seen
particularly good productions there. The choice of plays is not always
very discreet, and the acting is sometimes very poor, but the fact
remains that there exists a large number of intelligently enthusiastic
amateur groups, and there exists no organisation to exploit the connection between these groups and the professional theatre. English
amateurs have a valuable central organisation in England in the
British Drama League ; and in Scotland, where there is an equally
vigorous amateur movement, there is a similar organisation called
The Scottish Community Drama Association. These arrange an
annual competition for the performance of one-act plays, run on the
lines of a knock-out tournament. Last year the entries numbered
many hundreds, and the quality of the finalists was up to a good

professional standard in performance, and higher than any commercial standard in programme. In addition to the competition and the advantages of centralised organisation, the British Drama League and the Scottish Community Drama Association provide library facilities, lecture courses, and periodical " schools " with professional actors and producers to give lectures and take rehearsals. This instructional work would be immensely facilitated by a working connection with a professional theatre, and could by this means be extended to provide what amateurs most urgently need : an opportunity for their producers to acquire, under professional guidance, first-hand experience of professional rehearsal.

Members of amateur groups, connected with a professional theatre as agents, would have, as it were, a finger in both pies, and would form an automatically organised link between the two, cognisant of the needs of both, and able to exploit the possibilities of co-operation to their very considerable mutual advantage.

VII

ORGANISATION BEHIND THE CURTAIN .

BEFORE any attempt can be made to organise an audience for serious plays it would be necessary for the manager of a theatre to have clear-cut plans about the organisation of the programme and the company.

VIII

PROGRAMME : NEW PLAYS VERSUS CLASSICAL REVIVALS

SUCH a manager has the choice of three classes of programme. In the first place, he can confine himself to classical revivals : the policy, for instance, of the Old Vic and Sadler's Wells in London ; although

perhaps a theatre with a guaranteed audience would be expected by its patrons to provide a more catholic programme of revivals than does the Vic-Wells company, which is, admittedly and very rightly, concerned almost entirely with Shakespeare. Such a policy would, at least, be unimpeachable on grounds of taste, and unassailable by the cinema, which can only offer adaptations of classical works. But a programme exclusively of revivals tends to be a trifle musty, a trifle worthy, to savour a trifle of University Extension ; and a season which did not include any expression of contemporary thought and contemporary technique (except in the interpretation of classics) would not attract the support of youthful and enterprising spirits.

On the other hand, a programme entirely composed of new plays entails still greater drawbacks. For one thing it is far more risky. Even the most discriminating reader makes mistakes at times and recommends for production plays which are wholly unsuitable. Also the actual preparation for a production is a far more risky business with a new play than with an old. Of necessity the script of a play suffers a sea-change during its first passage from the study to the stage. Cuts are made, new lines inserted, business altered ; and it must be remembered that the classics have not only been through this process but have stood the acid test of performance, and that what we have before us are, with a very few exceptions, not merely acting versions but acted versions. Furthermore, around most of them there have grown acting traditions, and although these are often clichés and may be often wisely disregarded, they are still useful guide-posts, indicating not only what previous actors have done with a scene, but what previous audiences have enjoyed. There is the further drawback that the supply of unperformed plays, of a standard to satisfy a discriminating audience, is extremely limited and, with the increasing inducements of the cinema and other dramatic media, is likely to become more so. Thus the audience that subscribes to a season of new plays will be speculating heavily upon the good taste, good judgment, and good luck of the management. Finally, the same drawback applies to an exclusively new programme as, conversely, to one exclusively of revivals : the youthful and enterprising may

support it, but Colonel Slocum and the Biddulph girls, earnest and intelligent, will stay away.

There remains the third alternative, a mixture of old and new. This would seem to be the wisest course, since it affronts neither conservative nor radical taste, and would enable the theatre to leaven the classical lump with productions of good new plays which need not be so frequent as to exceed the supply.

Thus the supply of new plays would condition the number of their productions compared to the number of classical revivals.

IX

RESPONSIBILITY FOR SELECTING PLAYS

IT is possible for the selection of plays to lie in the hands of one person or of many. The season ticket holders might claim that as the financial mainstay of the scheme they had a right to the selection by a system of plebiscite. In the case of new plays, the circulation of the script among several thousand subscribers, the collation of several thousand opinions, render it almost impracticable. In addition it would take the gilt considerably off the gingerbread of a first production if all the subscribers were familiar with the script before ever they came to the theatre. In the case of classical revivals a modified form of plebiscite is practicable. The management can offer to their subscribers a list of possible revivals and guarantee to produce those which obtain the largest number of votes. The scheme has advantages. It enables the management to gauge to some extent the taste of the subscribers, and it makes the season tickets more attractive by conferring an additional privilege upon their holders. The principal drawback is that, as in every democratic constitution, only the numerical majority will get their views represented ; and the majority tends to be the less well informed and less discriminating portion of the community. But if this drawback makes itself felt to what, in the view of the management, is the genuine

XII *ABOVE*

Miss Marie Tempest and Mr. Henry Ainley in " The First
Mrs. Fraser " by St. John Ervine : two magnetic stars in an
eminently successful comedy

BELOW

The Compagnie des Quinze in " Le Viol de Lucrece " by
Andre Obey : no stars, no scenery, precious little " box-office
appeal," but an influence that is already fertile

ABOVE : Reproduced by permission of Sasha, photographer

BELOW : *Reproduced by permission of Bronson Albery, Esq., and Pollard
Crowther, Esq., photographer*

86

XI   Shavian St. Joan :   Dame Sybil Thorndike

Reproduced by permission of Pollard Crowther, photographer

84

X Two Romantic St. Joans

Miss Huddart, riding apparently to Banbury Cross

Mrs. Baddeley as La Pucelle in Shakespeare's " Henry VI "

Both reproduced by permission from the " Gabrielle Enthoven " collection at the Victoria and Albert Museum

ERRATUM

Page 80 should read :—

ABOVE
Mr. Nugent Monck's setting, *etc*.

BELOW
Mr. Terence Gray's interpretation, *etc*.

IX   Production of Shakespeare

ABOVE
Mr. Terence Gray's interpretation of " Romeo and Juliet "
at the Festival Theatre, Cambridge

BELOW
Mr. Nugent Monck's setting for " Othello " at the Maddermarket Theatre, Norwich

Reproduced by permission of the Festival and Maddermarket Theatres

VIII Production of Shakespeare

" Hamlet " produced in modern dress by H. K. Ayliff for the Birmingham Repertory Theatre

Reproduced by permission of the Birmingham Repertory Theatre

VIII   Production of Shakespeare

" Hamlet " produced in modern dress by H. K. Ayliff for the
Birmingham Repertory Theatre

Reproduced by permission of the Birmingham Repertory Theatre

IX Production of Shakespeare

ABOVE
Mr. Terence Gray's interpretation of " Romeo and Juliet "
at the Festival Theatre, Cambridge

BELOW
Mr. Nugent Monck's setting for " Othello " at the Maddermarket Theatre, Norwich

Reproduced by permission of the Festival and Maddermarket Theatres

XII *ABOVE*

Miss Marie Tempest and Mr. Henry Ainley in " The First Mrs. Fraser " by St. John Ervine : two magnetic stars in an eminently successful comedy

BELOW

The Compagnie des Quinze in " Le Viol de Lucrece " by Andre Obey : no stars, no scenery, precious little " box-office appeal," but an influence that is already fertile

XI   Shavian St. Joan : Dame Sybil Thorndike

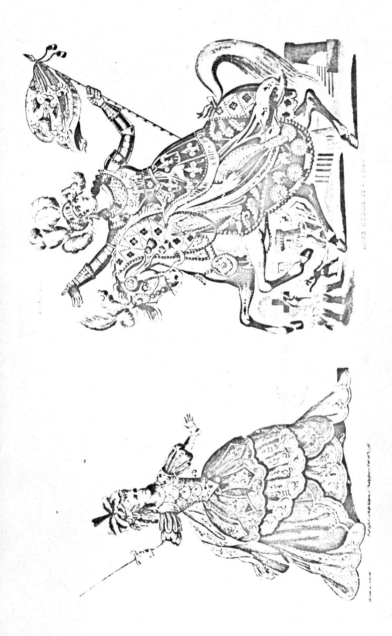

X Two Romantic St. Joans

RIGHT
Miss Huddart, riding apparently to Banbury Cross

LEFT
Mrs. Baddeley as La Pucelle in Shakespeare's " Henry VI "

Both reproduced by permission from the " Gabrielle Enthoven " collection at the Victoria and Albert Museum

82